# ALASKA

*A Sunset Pictorial*

# ALASKA

LANE PUBLISHING CO. • MENLO PARK, CALIFORNIA

*Edited by*
Dorothy Krell

*Design*
Joe Seney

*Cartography and Illustrations*
Dick Cole

*Editor, Sunset Books*
David E. Clark

Fifth Printing February 1980
Copyright © Lane Publishing Co.,
Menlo Park, California.
First Edition 1974. World rights reserved. No part of
this publication may be reproduced by any
mechanical, photographic, or electronic process, or
in the form of a phonographic recording, nor may it
be stored in a retrieval system, transmitted, or
otherwise copied for public or private use without
prior written permission from the publisher.
Library of Congress No. 73-89568. ISBN 0-376-
05154-X. Lithographed in the United States.

# Contents

Front cover: Naknek Lake, Katmai National Monument; photograph by Nancy Simmerman. Back cover: North American Sled
Dog Championship Races, Fairbanks; photograph by G. C. Kelley. Title page: Mount McKinley, photograph by Willis Peterson.
Photographs credited to the University of Washington Press are from the book *One Man's Gold Rush* by Murray Morgan.

# A Beckoning Frontier

Alaska has wilderness, wildlife, fishing, glaciers, tundra. It has old Russian churches, Eskimo villages, fiords, totem poles, permafrost, northern lights, and midnight sun. It is so vast that it is difficult to comprehend its size. The big states of Texas, California, and Montana combined would fit easily in its 586,400 square miles. If a map of Alaska were superimposed on a map of the rest of the United States mainland, it would blanket the central part of the country from the Canadian border to Arkansas and from Indiana to Colorado. Its southeastern corner would reach to the Atlantic Coast, and its Aleutian Islands would extend beyond the Pacific Coast.

It is not surprising that in so huge an area there are regions that differ distinctly—in climate, scenery, people, topography, and economy. Alaska divides naturally into six such regions: Southeastern Alaska, often referred to as "the Panhandle"; the Interior, bounded by the Alaska Range on the south and the Brooks Range on the north; the Southcentral region, rimming the Gulf of Alaska south of the Alaska Range; Southwestern Alaska, extending from the Alaska Peninsula to the tip of the Aleutian Islands; the Western coastal area, bordering the Bering Sea; and the Arctic, above the Arctic Circle.

Southeastern Alaska is a tourist's paradise, made up of several large islands, hundreds of smaller ones, and a thin strip of rugged mainland bordering Canada. Jagged mountains rise from picturesque fiords along the protected waterway called the Inside Passage, and glaciers reach to the water's edge. Most of the Southeast is part of Tongass National Forest. Massive stands of spruce, hemlock, and cedar cover the islands and much of the mainland. Juneau, Alaska's capital, hugs the mountains near the northern end of the waterway. Most of the other Panhandle towns are engaged in fishing and lumbering

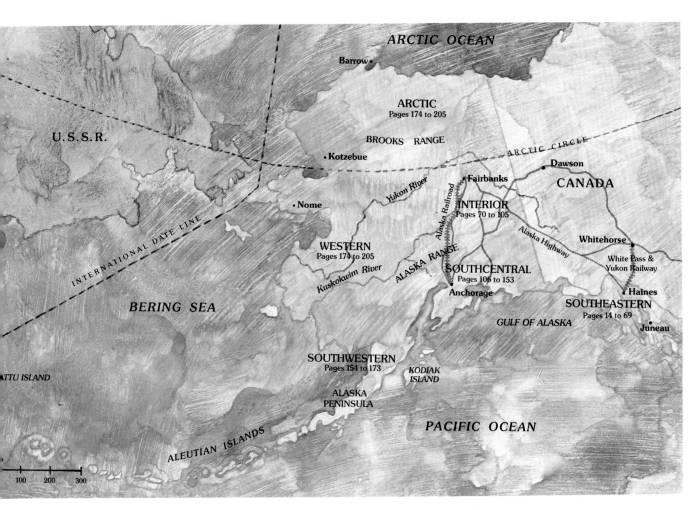

THE ALEUTS CALLED IT ALASHKA, or "The Great Land." A giant
of a state, Alaska has one-fifth the land mass of the continental
United States. Four time zones lie within its borders, and its Aleutian
Islands extend into the Eastern Hemisphere.

activities. No roads connect the towns along the
waterway. The ferries of the Alaska Marine Highway
System are the principal inter-city transportation. Jet
aircraft connect the Southeast with the rest of Alaska and
with the other states, and small planes reach out in all
directions to serve otherwise isolated communities. Cruise
ships ply the waterway in summer. This part of Alaska
has a maritime climate, with cold winters, cool summers,
frequent fogs, and heavy rains—more than 150 inches a
year in some places.

   Alaska's Interior is a huge, rolling upland, bordered by
the Alaska Range to the south and the Brooks Range to
the north. It stretches from the Canadian border almost
to the Bering Sea and is drained by the mighty Yukon
and Kuskokwim rivers which, fed by many tributaries,

wind through this region to their outlets at the Bering Sea. Much of the Interior is uninhabited. Fairbanks, Alaska's second largest city, is trade center for the region. Elsewhere, settlements are tiny and scattered. Wildlife is abundant here, and the great preserve of Mount McKinley National Park is a major tourist destination. Summers in the Interior are warm. In winter, temperatures plummet—sometimes to 60 and 70 degrees below zero. (The coldest winter temperature ever recorded in Alaska was −80 degrees at Prospect Creek, about 150 miles northwest of Fairbanks.)

Half of Alaska's people live in the Southcentral part of the state, which borders the Gulf of Alaska south of the Alaska Range and includes Prince William Sound, Cook Inlet, and the Kenai Peninsula. At the center of this region is Anchorage, Alaska's largest city. Seward and Whittier are principal access ports for the Alaska Railroad. Valdez will be the seaport terminus for the 800-mile-long pipeline that will bring oil from the North Slope to Prince William Sound. The Kenai Peninsula, a favorite vacation destination for many Alaskans, is also an important oil-producing region; Alaska's first producing oil and gas wells were drilled on the shore and beneath the waters of Cook Inlet. North of Anchorage, the fertile Matanuska Valley is Alaska's richest farming area. Skiing, fishing, hunting, and boating lie within easy reach of Southcentral cities. Picnicking and camping sites, hiking trails, and forest cabins are attractions on Chugach National Forest lands that border Prince William Sound. The climate of the Southcentral region is milder than that of the Interior; temperatures in the winter hover just above and below zero, and summers are cool and comfortable.

Southwestern Alaska is a long, narrow region that includes the Alaska Peninsula, the Aleutian Islands, and the Kodiak Island group. The Alaska Peninsula extends out into the Pacific Ocean for a distance of about 550 miles. From it, the Aleutians string out for an additional 1,500 miles. This is one of the "weather kitchens" of the Northern Hemisphere. Sudden storms brewed here affect the weather of all North America. The Southwestern region is mountainous and mostly treeless. Kodiak, the first permanent Russian settlement in Alaska, is the largest town in this part of the state. Military installations and a few isolated fishing villages are situated along the Aleutian chain.

The Bering Sea coastal area, the numerous offshore islands, and the Arctic region north of the Brooks Range are the homes of the Eskimos—hardy, friendly people who have survived in this rugged part of the world for centuries. Nome is the principal trading center for the Western region. Barrow, facing the Arctic Ocean at the top of the state, is Alaska's largest Eskimo village and a trading center for the far north. Arctic Alaska is a region of low precipitation, strong winds, cold winters, and cool summers.

Alaska was discovered in 1741 by Russian explorers led by Vitus Bering, a Dane in the service of Czar Peter the Great, but the first arrivals to Alaska came long before the 18th century. Anthropologists believe that the first Alaskans crossed over from Asia more than twelve thousand years ago by a land bridge that once connected the two continents. The Alaskan natives of today, descendants of these first tribes, comprise about one-sixth of the state's population. They are the Eskimos of the far north and the western coast, the Athabascan Indians of the Interior, the Indians of the Southeast, and the Aleuts of the Aleutian Islands.

The Aleuts, the first Alaskans to come in contact with the Europeans, were soon subjugated by Russian fur traders who made their headquarters in Southwestern Alaska.

When European explorers first set eyes on the magnificent mountains and forested shores of Southeastern Alaska, the Tlingit, Haida, and Tsimshian Indians had already become established there. Their culture had reached a high peak when Russian fur traders

NATIVE ALASKANS are the Tlingit, Haida, and Tsimshian Indians of the Southeast; the Athabascan Indians of the Interior; the Eskimos of the Bering Sea and Arctic coasts; and the Aleuts of the Aleutian Islands and the Alaska Peninsula.

NANCY SIMMERMAN

*AT SUNSET, a lone fishing boat heads for home port on quiet Inside Passage waters.*

discovered the wealth of marten, mink, and otter among the islands of the Inside Passage.

Ships captained by world-renowned explorers began to sail the coastal waters in the late 1700s, and Russian, British, and American traders vied for transportation rights on the Stikine and Taku rivers flowing from Canada. With the purchase of Alaska by the United States in 1867 (for $7.2 million, or about two cents an acre), settlers of many origins began coming north. Canneries were built; towns took shape. Gold strikes in Canada's Cassiar and Stikine districts in the early 1870s and near Juneau in 1880 brought an influx of miners.

As early as 1872, prospectors had discovered small amounts of gold in Canada's Yukon Territory, but it was not until 1896, when rich deposits began to show on Bonanza Creek, a tributary of the Klondike River, that the rush north began. Gold-laden steamers began returning to West Coast ports from the Yukon in the summer of 1897. First to arrive was the *Excelsior*, which steamed into San Francisco in July carrying about $400,000 in gold. Two days later, the *Portland* put into Seattle with about $700,000 in gold. When word of these fabulous cargoes spread throughout the world, the rush was on. Seattle, Portland, San Francisco, and Vancouver bustled with fortune-seekers impatient to start the great adventure.

*SNOWY PUFFS of Arctic cotton soften Alaska's fields in summer.*

Most of the gold-hungry hordes that streamed into the Yukon followed one of two routes: an all-water route around the southwestern tip of Alaska to the Bering Sea and then up the Yukon River; or a combination sea and overland route via the Inside Passage to Dyea or Skagway and the Chilkoot and White passes. The latter was by far the most popular choice. Ships deposited the miners at the head of the Lynn Canal—at Dyea or nearby Skagway. From Dyea, the gold seekers headed for Chilkoot Pass; from Skagway, the mountain crossing was through White Pass. At Lake Bennett, on the other side of the mountains, the miners again took to the water, this time in boats built from timbers cut on the spot or from boards laboriously and expensively hauled over the passes. Their arduous journey continued for 500 more miles, over a chain of lakes and hazardous rapids on the Yukon's headwaters to Dawson City, where the Klondike River entered the Yukon. The monumental task of building a much-needed railroad over the mountains began in May 1898. Two years later, the 111-mile rail link was completed, joining Skagway. via White Pass with Whitehorse in the Yukon Territory.

The Klondike Gold Rush came to an end soon after the turn of the century, but it was followed by a rush to Nome when gold was discovered on Anvil Creek and in

the beach sands of the Seward Peninsula. Another series of gold discoveries lured miners to the Fairbanks region between 1900 and 1910.

In 1912, Alaska was granted territorial status. On June 30, 1958, after a long battle for statehood, Congress approved legislation making Alaska the 49th state. The legislation was ratified by Alaska's voters in November, and on January 3, 1959, President Dwight Eisenhower officially proclaimed Alaska a state of the Union.

Most of the original sourdoughs who came to Alaska to seek their fortunes are gone. The gold rush brought a pioneering people to tame the land and develop its riches. World War II emphasized Alaska's strategic military position. Since that time, Alaska has remained a vital segment in our national defense system.

Alaska is now enjoying its biggest visitor rush. Once considered isolated and remote, this northernmost state is now an air crossroads for domestic and foreign flights. Bus tours bring summer visitors up the Alaska Highway. Cruise ships ply the Inside Passage. State ferries take visitors and their cars to places highways don't reach.

Like the rest of the world, Alaska is changing rapidly. Its environmental questions—especially the oil pipeline between the North Slope and the south coast—have made headlines in recent years. Under the Alaska Native Claims Settlement Act, signed into law in 1971, some 80 million acres of the state are now under study for possible use as national parks, national forests, and wildlife refuges. Alaska's native population will share in the revenue from the development of their state's resources.

The opportunities in Alaska challenge men's spirits. Those who have taken up the challenge have led Alaska to the threshold of the greatest economic development in the United States today. The pioneer spirit that recalls the vigor of a young America is still there; yet the Alaska of today is a different kind of frontier. The people who have learned to live in and enjoy this rugged land are as energetic, enthusiastic, self-reliant, and optimistic as those who came ahead of them. But they have had an opportunity to plan carefully for the future development of their state and to learn from the mistakes of others so that this exciting, almost untapped wilderness—the last such area in our United States—will be well used.

*SPLENDID ANIMALS roam Alaska's great expanses of wilderness. This caribou is silhouetted against Mount Mather in Mt. McKinley National Park.*

# The Southeast's Panhandle

# Fiords and forests and a marine highway to friendly towns

Alaska's southeastern corner, its so-called "Panhandle," is a special world of blue-green waterways and forested islands. Picturesque fiords cut deep into spectacular snow and ice-clad mountains that rise abruptly almost from the water's edge, and a remarkable collection of glaciers is born in the glistening icefields that drape the summits of the Coast Mountains. The sheltered waters of the Inside Passage have been a well-promoted route to the north for decades. In the late 1800s, side-wheelers and sternwheelers brought tourists from West Coast ports on the scenic voyage to Alaska and deposited gold-hungry miners at Skagway and Dyea, where they began their arduous trek to the Klondike gold fields. The vessels that ply the Inside Passage today offer comforts and conveniences undreamed of then. Now planes link friendly towns along the route. A railroad whisks passengers over the White Pass, following closely the rugged route taken by thousands of fortune seekers in the winter of 1897-98, and backpackers clamber over a well-marked but still wild and undeveloped Chilkoot Pass. Around you most of the time as you travel the waterway is forest wilderness, usually very close, interrupted only occasionally by photogenic towns compact enough to explore on foot in a few hours but fascinating enough to keep you for a longer stay. Wildlife abounds. Bald eagles perch high in treetops or soar on prevailing winds, for this is one of their major habitats. Bears roam the shoreline, and mountain goats climb lofty crags. Juneau, Alaska's capital city, nestles between steep mountains near the northern end of the Passage. Other smaller cities are engaged in fishing and lumbering, and all host a growing number of visitors who arrive from the "Lower 48."

MARTIN LITTON

# An Island-Studded Marine Highway

## Water link to isolated towns, and a popular tourist route for almost a century

*YOU TRAVEL IN COMFORT by modern ferry, luxurious cruise ship, or fast jet plane to the once-isolated Panhandle towns. In the 1890's, sidewheelers and sternwheelers, jammed to capacity with gold-hungry hordes bound for the Klondike, used this protected water route north from Seattle, Tacoma, Port Townsend, and Victoria. The mode of travel has improved, but the majestic vistas and rugged wilderness remain almost unchanged.*

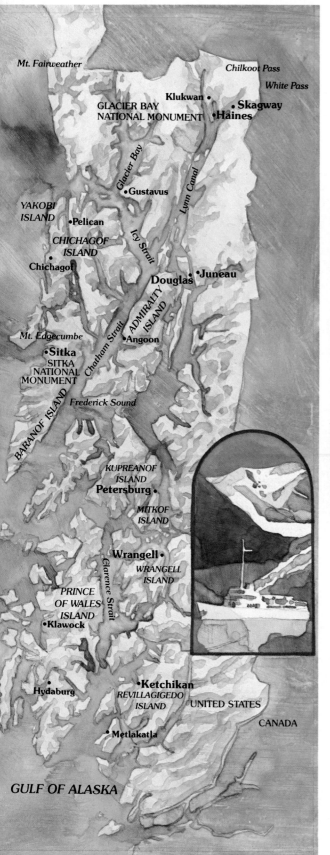

Mt. Fairweather

Chilkoot Pass

White Pass

GLACIER BAY
NATIONAL MONUMENT

Klukwan •

• Skagway

• Haines

Glacier Bay

Lynn Canal

• Gustavus

YAKOBI
ISLAND

• Pelican

Icy Strait

CHICHAGOF
ISLAND

Chichagof

Douglas •

• Juneau

Mt. Edgecumbe

ADMIRALTY
ISLAND

• Sitka

Chatham Strait

SITKA
NATIONAL
MONUMENT

• Angoon

BARANOF ISLAND

Frederick Sound

KUPREANOF
ISLAND

Petersburg •

MITKOF
ISLAND

Wrangell •

WRANGELL
ISLAND

Clarence Strait

PRINCE
OF WALES
ISLAND

• Klawock

• Hydaburg

• Ketchikan

REVILLAGIGEDO
ISLAND

UNITED STATES

CANADA

• Metlakatla

GULF OF ALASKA

# ...Marine Highway

DON NORMARK

*FROM PRINCE RUPERT TO SKAGWAY,
the Marine Highway winds through a maze of
waterways sheltered from the ocean by a huge
archipelago of forested islands that extends for
some 500 miles. The Haines ferry landing near
the northern end of the Inside Passage is one of
two places where a water journey northward can end
and a land journey into the Interior can begin.
The other is Skagway, where the narrow-gauge White
Pass & Yukon Railway carries passengers, cars,
and freight between Skagway and Whitehorse in
Canada's Yukon Territory.*

CHUCK DIVEN

*ALL MANNER OF CRAFT enliven the scene, but what may impress you most is the closeness of mountains and tidewater. Ice-clad mountains begin almost at the water's edge and form a magnificent backdrop to beautiful fiords, bays, and inlets, and occasional picturesque towns.*

DON NORMARK

# Ports of Call with Personality
## Tucked between mountains and tidewater, each has a character all its own

*SOUTHERNMOST PANHANDLE CITY, Ketchikan, above, clings to the slopes of Deer Mountain on Revillagigedo Island. Steep streets and wooden stairways climb to hill-hanging homes that overlook town and harbor. The unhurried routine of the Wrangell fisherman, opposite, typifies the slow-paced life in towns all over Southeastern Alaska and the marine-oriented activity that makes wandering along their waterfronts a fascinating pastime.*

# Alaska's Little Norway

*FOUNDED BY Norwegian fishermen, tidy Petersburg shows its Scandinavian background in colorfully painted houses, gay gardens, annual Norwegian Festival.*

# An Enthusiastic Greeting
Frontier informality combines with
true Alaska friendliness

*ALWAYS HAPPY TO SEE YOU, the town of Wrangell turns out en masse when cruise ships arrive. The Wrangell High School band has been greeting new arrivals exuberantly for about fifteen years. Wrangell, strategically located at the mouth of the navigable Stikine River, has been a Russian fort, Hudson's Bay Company post, and the U. S. Army's Fort Wrangell.*

*DOCKSIDE ACTIVITIES offer lively subject matter for photographers. Enterprising youngsters greet new arrivals with a warm welcome and an intriguing assortment of wares, ranging from wildflowers to garnets from the Stikine River delta area. In top photo, an amused visitor is the recipient of a badge reading, "I've been to Wrangell, Alaska."*

# Last Russian Headquarters
## Historic Sitka . . . for six decades it was Russia's New World capital

*THE PORT OF SITKA was the busiest and most promising city on the Pacific Coast in 1848, when the Russian Orthodox cathedral called St. Michael's was completed. The cathedral in the heart of old Sitka, above, was an active church and symbol of Alaska's Russian era until a fire in 1966 destroyed it and one-fifth of Sitka's business district. Now being restored, it will soon again house a valuable collection of icons and artifacts depicting Alaska's Russian-American history. Log building in photograph is the Sitka Trading Company, Russian-built and known as the Trading Post. Pacific Coast Steamship Company flag indicates that a steamer of that company was in port when photograph was taken.*

CHARLES WECKLER

TIM THOMPSON

*RUSSIAN CEMETERY is dominated by above replica of an old Russian blockhouse, typical of those in the stockade that rimmed Sitka during tense times under Russian rule. A battle fought at Sitka in 1804 between the Russians and the Tlingit Indians won for Russia an overseas empire which it retained until ownership of Alaska was transferred to the United States in October, 1867.*

# ...Sitka

AN IDEAL ANCHORAGE, Sitka's protected offshore waters sheltered the first trading ships of the Russian-American empire. Now car ferries bring visitors to this compact city on Baranof Island, and pleasure craft like the one above are a vital part of the waterfront scene.

NEW ARCHANGEL DANCERS *whirl through the intricate steps of a Russian folk dance. The colorfully costumed group, which performs for Sitka visitors, is comprised entirely of local women. Their repertoire includes 22 authentic dances from various parts of Russia.*

# Salmon is Number One

## Halibut, shrimp, and crab are runners-up

TIM THOMPSON

*DRIPPING NETS of salmon (right) and tiny, flavorful shrimp (below) are hauled aboard boats near Petersburg. Though the catch is mostly seasonal (sometimes 60 percent of the entire year's salmon catch will be landed in one month), fishing remains the state's second major industry, surpassed only by petroleum.*

TIM THOMPSON

*TWO WEEKS' CATCH of halibut being unloaded at Petersburg's cold storage plant may make you wonder why you ever bothered to go deep-sea fishing at home. Most Pacific halibut caught today come from Alaska's coastal waters. Some weigh 100, 200, or even 300 pounds.*

# Multimillion Dollar Industry
## It calls for the special skills of robust men

*LOG BRONCS scoot through the jam at Wrangell mill, Alaska's largest sawmill. Most of Southeastern Alaska is part of the Tongass National Forest, and the great stands of spruce, hemlock, and cedar that blanket most of the land are one of the state's most valued resources.*

*ROUGH-AND-READY loggers are an ever-present part of the scene in Southeastern Alaska. In annual logging championship events, loggers compete in chopping, pole climbing, choker-setting (below), sawing, and other skills essential to their jobs.*

# A Legacy from the Past

TOM TRACY

*TOTEM BIGHT PARK near Ketchikan displays a collection of poles and a traditional long house set up on what was for many years a favorite Tlingit campsite—an open meadow above a curve of fine gravel beach, ideal for landing or launching canoes.*

# Unique Southeastern attractions,
# carved by master craftsmen

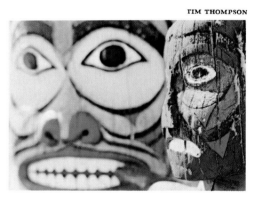

*LEGENDS, EVENTS, STORIES
are related by totemic figures
on poles. Old poles like the
beautifully weathered Kik sadi
pole at top left are sometimes
most fascinating of all.
Early carvers used paints made
by age-old methods: white from
ground clam shells, black from
charcoal or lignite coal, red from
hematite or red ferric oxide,
blue-green from copper. Bright,
enamel-like paints sometimes used
today more often than not obscure
and detract from the carvings.*

# Where Eagles Fly
## More bald eagles than all the other states combined

*PRIME HABITAT for bald eagles is the forested coastline and offshore islands of Southeastern Alaska. One of the heaviest concentrations occurs around the 678-mile coastline of Admiralty Island, which averages almost two nests per mile. The Chilkat Valley near Haines is another favorite area. White headfeathers gave this regal bird its name. The term "bald" was commonly used during the 17th and 18th centuries to signify white.*

EAGLE NEST TREES are usually located in old-growth timber, often in the upper third of old conifers or in crotches of large cottonwood trees. The birds return to the nest year after year, adding new material each time the nest is used. Nests sometimes are five to seven feet deep and six to eight feet in diameter and may contain as much as 150 cubic feet of limbs, twigs, moss, and grass. Nest building begins in early April, and by the end of July most of the eaglets are ready to fly.

FRED C. ROBARDS

JIM REARDEN

# Just Behind Juneau
## An ice reservoir feeds blue-white glaciers behind Alaska's hill-hugging capital

*A CITY WAS SURE TO GROW, even here on the confining slope at the foot of towering Mount Juneau, when Dick Harris and Joe Juneau found gold in Gold Creek in 1880. Their strike was the start of a fabulous gold-producing era during which more than $150 million in gold was taken from the mines around present-day Juneau.*

*KNIFE-EDGE PEAKS, called "nunataks," jut from immeasurable fields of hardened ice in the Juneau Icefields that cover some 1,500 square miles from the Taku River in the south to the Skagway River in the north. Spectacular flightseeing tours over the immense fields are popular excursions from Juneau and offer an experience not easily forgotten.*

# ...Juneau

*OLD AND NEW combine in this modern city where the spirit of early Alaska is still reflected in turn-of-the-century homes, winding streets, and frontier-style bars. Old houses at left contrast sharply with modern Federal Office Building. The tiny Russian Orthodox Church above was built in the late 1800's.*

# The Mendenhall...Accessible Glacier
## You can walk to it, climb above it, camp below it

KEITH GUNNAR

*A RETREATING GLACIER, the Mendenhall is melting back faster than it is flowing forward, but it is still an impressive sight. In bad weather, you can observe the glacier through the picture windows of a modern visitor center from which the easy path shown here leads to the lake.*

*WEST GLACIER TRAIL,*
*about three miles long,*
*climbs alongside the glacier,*
*tunneling through dense*
*growth, bridging musical*
*brooks, and crossing flowery*
*slopes, with clear views*
*over ice ridges and crevasses.*

*A CONVENIENT BASE for exploring*
*the Mendenhall is the improved*
*campground across the lake, near the*
*start of the West Glacier Trail.*
*In summer, the ground is colorfully*
*carpeted with purple lupine.*

# An Unassuming Roadhead

*FORMER OFFICERS QUARTERS line one side of parade ground at old Fort Seward in Haines. At crafts center here, students of Alaskan Indian art learn the ancient techniques used by the Tlingits to work designs in wood, silver, copper, jade, and soapstone. Totem carvers give demonstrations, and the Chilkat Dancers perform for visitors.*

# From quiet Haines, you can drive
# north to a much different world

*SNOWY MOUNTAINS tower more than 5,000 feet above Haines marina. From here, the unpaved Haines Highway connects with the Alaska Highway. During the gold rush, pack animals shipped from Seattle and Vancouver were driven from Haines over the old Dalton Trail to the Yukon.*

# Wilderness Beckons Beyond the Towns

Fishing lakes, quiet forests, and
untrampled shores are always close at hand

*TRANQUILITY reigns in the
Southeast's forests. Not
far from the few towns, a
fisherman can be almost
alone—except for an occasional
spying porcupine or a roaming
bear on the lookout for a salmon.*

*HIGH MOUNTAIN LAKE near Haines
is a quiet retreat for these two.
Mountain goats are sometimes seen
on these mountains, and moose
are occasional visitors to the lake.*

# Glacier Bay is Quiet Country
## Bigger than Yellowstone National Park, three times as big as Yosemite

RUTH KIRK

RUTH KIRK

*THE NATURE PHOTOGRAPHER can choose
from a range of subjects no matter what
the weather. Waterfowl are abundant on the
many coves and inlets. Ravens, ptarmigan,
and hummingbirds inhabit the shorelands.
Icebergs become marvelous sculptures and also
provide convenient beds for playful seals.*

*PLACID WATERS of Johns Hopkins
Inlet, left, mirror peaks that rise
from sea level to 7,000 feet within
four miles of the shore and supply
moisture to all the glaciers on the
peninsula that separates Glacier Bay
from the Gulf of Alaska.*

# Rivers of Ice
## Fifteen active glaciers reach tidewater

*FOUNTAINHEAD OF GLACIERS, 15,300-foot Mount Fairweather on horizon in photograph at right, marks the Alaska-Canada border, only 15 miles from the sea. Icefalls thousands of feet high on the near ridge feed Grand Pacific Glacier, one of 15 active tidewater glaciers in Glacier Bay National Monument.*

KEITH GUNNAR

*MUIR GLACIER, one of the most active on Alaska's coast, rises some 265 feet above the water and is nearly two miles wide. In 1899, John Muir had a cabin at the lower end of Muir Glacier. Since then, the glacier has receded 18 miles and cannot even be seen from the cabin site.*

MARTIN LITTON

*DEEPLY RIDGED surface of glacier shows in this closeup view. As a glacier reaches tidewater, water undermines ice fronts and huge chunks break loose to crash into the sea.*

FORESTS LAY BURIED, *perhaps for 3,000 years, when glaciers covered the land. Well-preserved stumps, many still in upright position, were exposed as the glaciers melted and their streams cut through the deep deposits of sand and gravel beneath the ice. Examples at right are just north of Fingers Bay in Glacier Bay National Monument*

SWEPT CLEAN *by a giant wave, Lituya Bay's shore lost nearly four square miles of forest in 1958. Triggered by an earthquake, ice crashed into the bay causing a wave 1,720 feet high to surge up on the opposite shore. Still several hundred feet high, it swept down the eight-mile length of the bay, stripping the shore as it went.*

# A Land Transformed

## In some places, the ice was more than four thousand feet deep

KEITH GUNNAR

*PLENTY OF OPEN SPACE attracts hikers to Glacier Bay National Monument. The couple above is following the quiet Bartlett River Trail. For wilderness camping at sites far up the bay and its tributaries, the daily cruise boat can drop you off and pick you up at a prearranged time.*

# Where the Waterway Ends
## Fortune called from beyond these mountains

UNIVERSITY OF WASHINGTON PRESS

WAGON ROAD THROUGH THE CUTOFF 3.6 MILES FROM THE SUMMIT OF

*AT THE END OF THE PASSAGE, the miners' trek to the gold fields began. The magnificent mountains that form a spectacular setting for the town of Skagway were a grim barrier for the thousands of gold-seekers who disembarked here and set out on the trail that was to become known as "Dead Horse Trail." (At one point on the trail, almost 3,000 pack animals were lost.) For all the towering grandeur of the ranges around this delightful town, Skagway is the only Southeastern Alaska town built on level ground—the flood plain of the Skagway River. Ferries and cruise ships tie up at docks in foreground; terminus of White Pass & Yukon Railway is at lower right.*

# ...Skagway

SKAGWAY'S BROADWAY is quiet now, but it was a different scene in 1898 when 20,000 fortune-seekers thronged the rip-roaring boom town at the start of the White Pass Trail. A living ghost town now, Skagway has about 700 residents who seek to retain the old-time flavor.

KEITH GUNNAR

MARTIN LITTON

WOODEN SIDEWALKS, unpaved streets, and false-front buildings, most of which are still in use, characterize the Skagway of today. Quiet for much of the year, the town livens up considerably when the summer tourists arrive.

# In the Steps of Adventurers

## Chilkoot Pass is still for foot travelers only

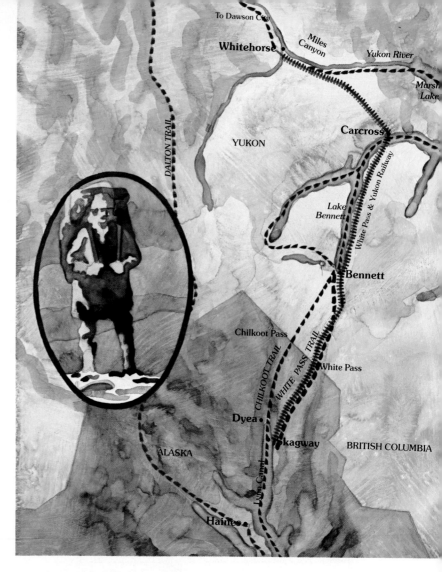

*FAMOUS TRAILS to the gold fields, above, included one that started from Dyea, near Skagway, and led over 3,739-foot Chilkoot Pass. The classic photograph at left, by gold rush photographer E. G. Hegg, shows the chain of heavily burdened miners climbing the 32-degree grade just below the summit. It was a climb up twelve hundred icy steps, and a man made many a trip before he got the last of his supplies to the top.*

*WET WEATHER is common on the south side of the pass, with possible freezing temperatures at night. The rusting donkey engine below, which powered an aerial tramway for the miners, is among relics hikers find along trail.*

*TODAY'S HIKERS follow a cleared and marked Chilkoot Trail. Most of the climb is easy going, but the final quarter mile to the summit is practically an all-fours ascent.*

# Rail Link to the Yukon

BUILDING THE RAILROAD was a challenging feat. Work began in May, 1898. The golden spike signifying completion of the route was hammered into place in July, 1900. In many places the track was laid right alongside the old trail followed by the sourdoughs. In top photo, all hands help clear the track after a storm on the summit. Construction crew at right is hacking out the route on Porcupine Hill. Without heavy equipment, building of the railroad was one of the most difficult of such projects ever engineered.

CLEARING THE TRACK AFTER A SNOW STORM ON THE SUMMIT OF WHITE PASS AND YUKON ROUTE, MAR. 20.

# Built at the peak of the Gold Rush, it's a scenic and a working line today

*CAMPERS, CARS, AND TRAILERS are secured to flatcars for the 110-mile White Pass & Yukon Railway trip between Skagway and Whitehorse, Yukon. Passengers view the rugged but beautiful scenery and remnants of the old Trail of '98 from comfortable chair cars.*

# The Run Downstream

One of the worst hazards
faced by the gold seekers of '98

SQUAW RAPIDS, BETWEEN MILES CANYON AND WHITE HORSE RAPIDS.    COPYRIGHT, 1898.

*DANGEROUS WHITE WATER of Miles Canyon and
the series of rapids below it wrecked 150 small boats
and took ten lives in a single week at the beginning
of the Klondike Gold Rush. After that week, the
Northwest Mounted Police halted all craft headed
downstream through this narrow, sheer-walled trap of
turbulent currents. Women and children were told
to get out and walk, the men to take aboard an
experienced helmsman. Now tourists can sample this
stretch of the Yukon River—but through quieter waters,
slowed by a dam built at Whitehorse Rapids in 1958.
The Schwatka, left, circles the lake formed by the dam
and continues upstream for 15 miles through Miles Canyon.*

# Destination Dawson

## Reminders of another era still exist in the Yukon Territory's "City of Gold"

UNIVERSITY OF WASHINGTON PRESS

MEN AND SUPPLIES *were everywhere in the Dawson of gold rush times. This 1899 photograph of Dawson's main street shows a pack train belonging to the Bartlett brothers, who for several years transported miners' goods from Dawson to the gold fields.*

*GOOD PHOTO SUBJECTS are easy to find near Dawson. The old store may be about to topple, but judging from his woodpile, the old-timer at right expects to be around a while longer.*

*PALACE GRAND THEATRE, built in 1899, has been given a face-lifting to greet today's tourists. Audiences view variety shows and melodramas reminiscent of gold rush days.*

# Today's Road North
## From Dawson Creek, B.C., to Fairbanks, Alaska…a 1,520-mile adventure

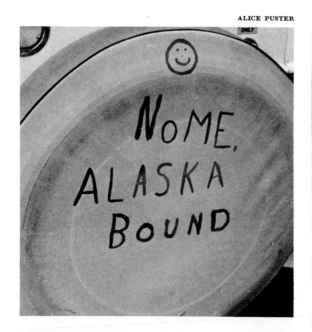

*A DUSTY DRIVE but not a hazardous one, if you plan carefully, the Alaska Highway is well-maintained but unpaved in Canada, black-topped in Alaska. The signs above sum up the spirit of adventure felt by those who travel it. It's obviously easier on four wheels than on two!*

# ...Alaska Highway

*OCTOBER SNOWFALL at Haines Junction whitens ground and trees and gently blankets the tiny church of "Our Lady of the Way." Made from an old Quonset hut, the little church is a landmark along the Alaska Highway. Though the highway is most traveled in summer, many veterans of the trip prefer the fall when traffic is light and the hillsides are ablaze with the golden color of aspen and birch.*

*INDIAN CEMETERY at Champagne
is a picturesque attraction along
the Alaska Highway. Champagne,
now abandoned, was a trading post on
the old Dalton Trail built by pioneer
Jack Dalton to move pack animals from
Haines to the Klondike. Log cabins
below still stand at nearby Silver
City, which was at various times
a trading post, roadhouse, and
Northwest Mounted Police barracks.*

# The Vast Interior

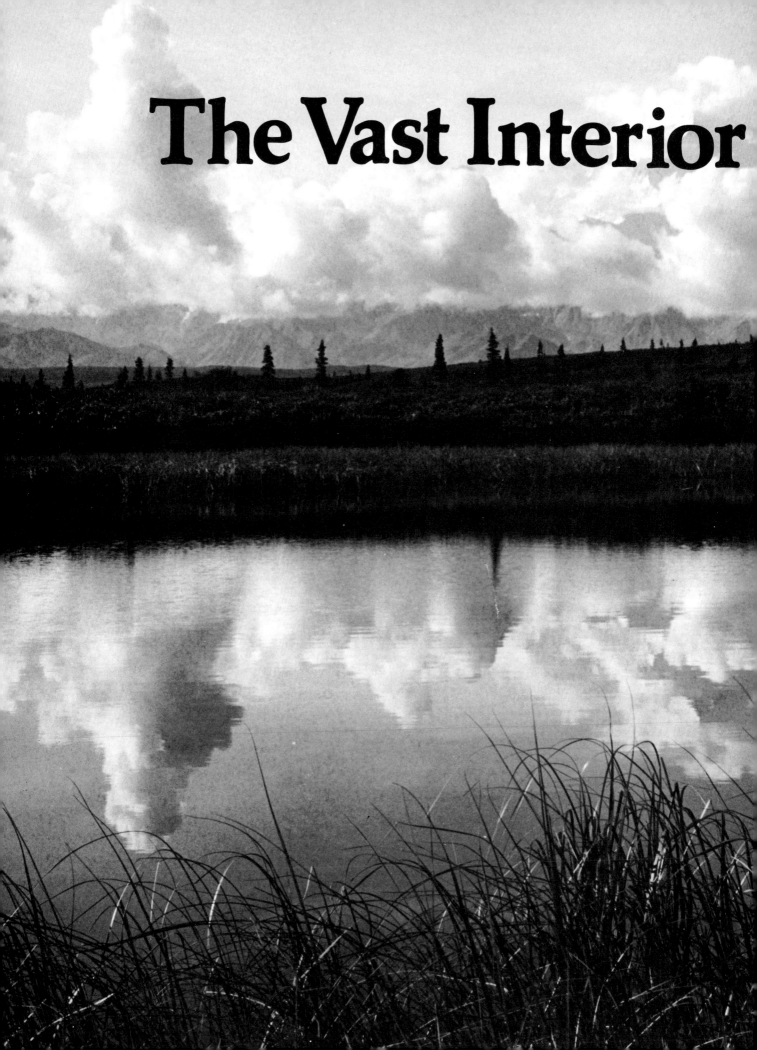

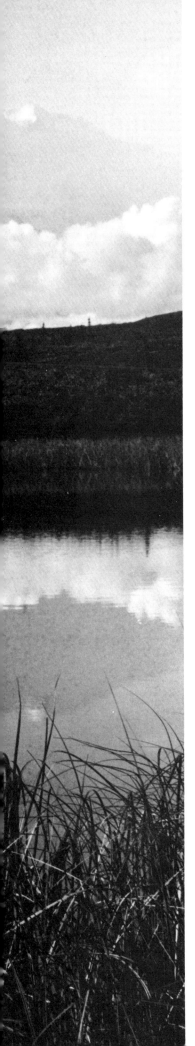

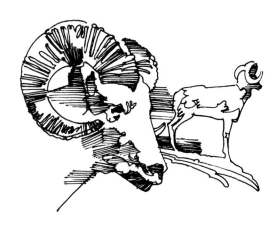

# Subarctic wilderness and a frontier city between majestic ranges

Two almost impenetrable barriers, the craggy Alaska Range at the south and the enormous bulk of the Brooks Range at the north, set off Alaska's Interior Plateau, a huge area of rolling uplands that extends from the Canadian border almost to the Bering Sea. The Yukon River and its tributaries wind through thousands of miles of this region to empty into the Bering Sea. Interior Alaska is the country of the Athabascan Indians. Many still subsist here by trapping, hunting, and fishing, but others have left their isolated villages for city life. Discovery of gold on the Forty-Mile in 1886 lured prospectors and miners to this part of Alaska even before the rush to the Klondike. Little Circle City, on the banks of the Yukon, boomed in 1895 when a gold discovery was made on Birch Creek. Fairbanks was born in 1902 when Felix Pedro found gold in the Tanana Valley. Now Fairbanks is Alaska's second largest city and combines a gold rush past with a twentieth-century present. Fairbanks is a place to see gold dredges, old log cabins, and sternwheelers; as the nearest supply center for the oil fields on the North Slope just 350 miles away, it is also a modern boom town. Almost half the military stationed in Alaska are at two large bases near Fairbanks. The University of Alaska has its main campus here. Two major highways, the Alaska Highway and the Fairbanks-to-Anchorage highway, link the Interior with Canada, the "Lower 48," and Southcentral Alaska. Southwest of Fairbanks, Mount McKinley National Park is one of the world's great wildlife preserves; reigning majestically above it is North America's highest mountain, 20,320-foot Mount McKinley. The great central plateau of Alaska is the coldest part of the state in the winter and the hottest in the summer. Winter temperatures often fall below zero—in some places to minus 60 or 70. Summer highs hover near 100 degrees.

PHILIP HYDE

# The Country Opens Up
## Vast vistas replace the coastal fiords

*THE MOOD IS EVER CHANGING.*
*Above, fireweed brightens the*
*summer landscape beneath a threatening*
*sky. At right, the alpine tundra*
*takes on subtle autumn hues.*

# A Lofty Barrier

*DRIFTING FOG hovers over the snowy Kahiltna Peaks, above, in this photograph taken from Windy Corner on Mount McKinley. Peak in upper right of photograph is 14,500-foot Mount Hunter. Aerial photograph at right shows Kichatna Spires in Alaska Range, southwest of Mount McKinley. Main peak in the group reaches 8,985 feet.*

# The summit peaks of Alaska's highest mountain range pierce the clouds

# Fairbanks is still the Frontier
## Modern city and hub of the Interior
## ...but the past is still in evidence

*ONE OF THE EARLIEST VIEWS of Fairbanks, above, was taken in June, 1904, soon after the name was changed from Barnette's Cache, the name of the trading post set up by Captain E. T. Barnette, an enterprising riverboat operator and trader. When Barnette's Cache became a boom camp, it was renamed for Charles Fairbanks, U.S. senator from Indiana and later vice president of the United States.*

*DOWNTOWN FAIRBANKS spreads out on both banks of the winding Chena River, a tributary of the Tanana, which in turn flows into the Yukon. The old gold dredge at right, no longer operating, stands as a reminder of the bygone era when Felix Pedro, an Italian immigrant, hit paydirt just outside of town.*

INTERIOR　　**77**

# ...Fairbanks

FORTY ACRES OF EXHIBITS and entertainment are the attractions at Alaskaland. Visitors can wander the streets of Gold Rush Town, below, created from relocated log cabins built during the gold rush days; climb aboard the old sternwheeler Nenana, right; pan for gold in Mining Valley; ride on the Crooked Creek & Whisky Island Line; or visit a native village of recreated early Eskimo and Indian dwellings.

*LITTLE CHANGED from its mining camp days, the Malemute Saloon*
*at Cripple Creek Resort is still in operation at Ester City on the Nenana*
*Road. Some claim that it was here at the Malemute that poet Robert*
*Service saw the shooting that inspired his famous "Shooting of Dan McGrew."*
*Although Service lived and wrote his northland poems in Dawson, Yukon,*
*his colorful ballads are told often in Alaska and are applauded*
*with enthusiasm by appreciative audiences.*

# Eerie Days, Ghostly Nights
## Ice fogs sometimes grip the land, but the winter skies offer exciting rewards

*FROZEN DROPS OF ICE hang in midair during a dismal Fairbanks ice fog, above. In a more welcome display, opposite, the northern lights (aurora borealis) sweep the sky like giant searchlights. Caused when the earth's upper atmosphere is bombarded by charged particles from the sun, they appear in a shimmering variety of colors and patterns.*

# The Winter Scene
## When temperatures plummet, snow sports come to the fore

BUD NELSON

CLIFF HOLLENBECK

WINTER FUN is different in the northland. Dog mushers come in all sizes and ages. Major event of the year is the North American Championship Dog Sled Races in March, but there's fun to be had in a minor way as the young lady at the left has discovered. Baseball is played the hard way during Fairbanks Winter Carnival. On June 21, a game is played without lights under the sun at midnight.

# Downriver by Sternwheeler
## You see the old and new Alaska on a thirty-mile back country cruise

JEFF PHILLIPS

*FIRST THE CHENA, then the Tanana, offer a look at the serene countryside just a few minutes from downtown Fairbanks. Berries, wild roses, aspen, juniper, and willows cover the shores. Swallows nest in eroded sand banks, and now and then a tepee-shaped beaver house comes into view. Two sternwheelers make the run, piloted by Captain Jim Binkley and his son. Their family has operated riverboats in Alaska since 1898.*

SOD-ROOFED trapper's cabin
and a modern floatplane base
are among the contrasts in scenery.
Along the Chena, friendly children
wave from modern homes along
the banks. You seem to leave
civilization behind as you
enter the wilder setting along
the Tanana.

# Farthest North University
## Special studies to meet Alaska's needs

*FROM SIX STUDENTS in 1922, the enrollment of the Fairbanks campus of the University of Alaska has grown to more than 3,000. In addition to the Fairbanks campus, the university operates four-year colleges in Anchorage and Juneau and eight community colleges throughout Alaska. The unusual building above and right is the William R. Wood Campus Activity Center, with copper-sheathed mall area, multilevel lounge, dining room, and recreational facilities*

DON WRIGHT

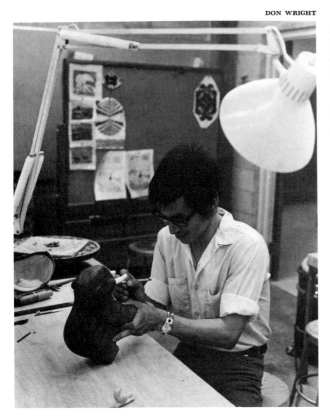

SPECIAL PROJECTS of the university
include the selective breeding of
musk ox at the university's musk ox farm
in an attempt to find a new economic
resource for native Alaskans in remote
villages. Qiviut, the downy undercoat
of the musk ox, is shed in spring,
then spun into a delicate yarn and
hand-knitted by Eskimo women into
luxurious garments. In another service,
artists and craftsmen with special talent
are trained in the use of wood, soapstone,
and silver, and the development of new
designs in a program supported in part
by grants from the Indian Arts and Crafts
Board and the Alaska State Council
on the Arts.

# Wonderful McKinley Park
## More than three thousand square miles, and almost all of it is wild country

MONARCH OF THE RANGE, North America's highest mountain reigns
majestically over a landscape of striking contrasts. The Indians called
the mountain Denali, "Home of the Sun," and the sunrise brightening Mount
McKinley in this view from Wonder Lake area seems to give merit to the title.

*THE ANIMAL LIFE is unsurpassed. Crags and mountain slopes are haven for the aristocratic Dall sheep (above). Most conspicuous evidence of the presence of a Toklat grizzly (left) is the small, crater-like holes made by the bears in digging out ground squirrels.*

# ...McKinley Park

*CURIOSITY brings twin fox pups out for a peek at a visitor and also gives the patient photographer at left a closeup view of a friendly Arctic ground squirrel. Caches like the one opposite, near the Toklat River, are used in many places in Alaska for safe food storage.*

# ...McKinley Park

UNEXPECTED CONTRASTS in the park are icy glaciers that descend from peaks in the Alaska Range and, at right, the brilliant colors of the volcanic cliffs at Polychrome Pass. The road that winds along the mountainside can be used by private vehicles by reservation only to reach campgrounds inside the park. Other park visitors use a shuttle bus to get around or can enjoy a conducted bus tour to view wildlife.

# ...McKinley Park

HIKERS HEAD OUT *across beautiful subarctic landscape. The few trails in the park are mostly short paths near the hotel. Elsewhere, serious hikers strike out over tundra or along gravel river bottoms. An easy day's hike through particularly beautiful country is along the trailless west shore of Wonder Lake, below. When clouds cooperate, the mountain looks close enough to touch.*

GLENN M. CHRISTIANSEN

G. C. KELLEY

*MORNING MIST floats among the spruce trees near Park Headquarters. The early-morning and late-afternoon hours are the best times for viewing the park's wildlife.*

# Nature's Changing Garb
## Sometimes meant to catch the eye, sometimes designed to fool it

*IT TAKES A SHARP EYE to spot the well-camouflaged ptarmigan. In summer, Alaska's state bird blends with the brown of the tundra. As winter approaches, it takes on the snowy white of its new background. The handsome male above is sporting his showy spring plumage.*

*A BRIEF BURST OF COLOR splashes the landscape with gold, which
all too soon will disappear beneath the first snows of a long winter.
Brilliant aspens above border Henderson Road on the way to Ester Dome.*

# Irresistible Challenge

ONE HUNDRED YARDS TO GO *before these climbers reach their goal—the summit of North America's highest mountain. Since McKinley's South Peak was first climbed on June 7, 1913, more than 300 people have successfully reached the 20,320-foot summit. Across Denali Pass, the mountain's North Peak, first climbed in 1910, is 850 feet lower.*

# An intrepid few cannot resist the lure of Mount McKinley's magnificent summit peaks

*GREAT CREVASSES impede climbers on Muldrow Glacier, above left, most frequently used route to South Peak. Sometimes these huge gaps can be safely crossed on snow bridges, but a detour is often the only way to the other side. Bands on the 60-foot-high ice blocks at right above show twelve seasons of snowfall.*

# Wilderness River
## Seemingly untouched by time, the mighty Yukon meanders lazily through a quiet land

*CIVILIZATION SEEMS FAR AWAY in this quiet scene along the Yukon. One of the great rivers of the world, the Yukon flows for about 2,000 miles and drains a watershed of more than 333,000 square miles.*

*PEACEFUL, PICTURESQUE,*
*and a favorite subject of*
*photographers, fish wheels still*
*turn quietly on many Alaskan*
*rivers, and the fish they trap*
*hang drying in the sun on the*
*river banks. Two paddleboards,*
*caught by the river's current,*
*keep the fish wheel in motion.*
*As one of its two mesh baskets*
*reaches a vertical position,*
*fish scooped up in it go sliding*
*down a slope board into the*
*waiting fish box set alongside*
*the ingenious contraption.*

# ...Yukon River

ALMOST FORGOTTEN NOW, the tiny village of Ruby on the Yukon's bank was a boom camp of more than 1,000 residents in 1907 during the frenzied rush to find gold in the streams that fed the river. Then the Yukon teemed with activity, but now the crowds have left, leaving the big cow moose at right to swim undisturbed.

*THOSE WHO STAY ON in the
quiet villages along the river
include some who stay by choice
and still prefer the simple
life of the past. At left, an
Athabascan woman at Galena
works patiently on a fish net.
A few, in the little Indian cemetery
at Cochrine, above, rest forever
on the Yukon's banks.*

# The Restless Caribou

## In thirteen major herds, they roam the tundra in much of the state

*CARIBOU KEEP MOVING in their constant search for food. In summer, they favor willow and birch leaves, grasses, and a variety of succulent plants. In winter, they search out lichens and dried sedges. Though their movements are extensive and unpredictable, they generally inhabit open tundra lands near or above timberline and travel hundreds of miles in their annual migrations. Cows and young move to the traditional calving grounds in spring and early summer. The bulls follow later, far to the rear and widely scattered.*

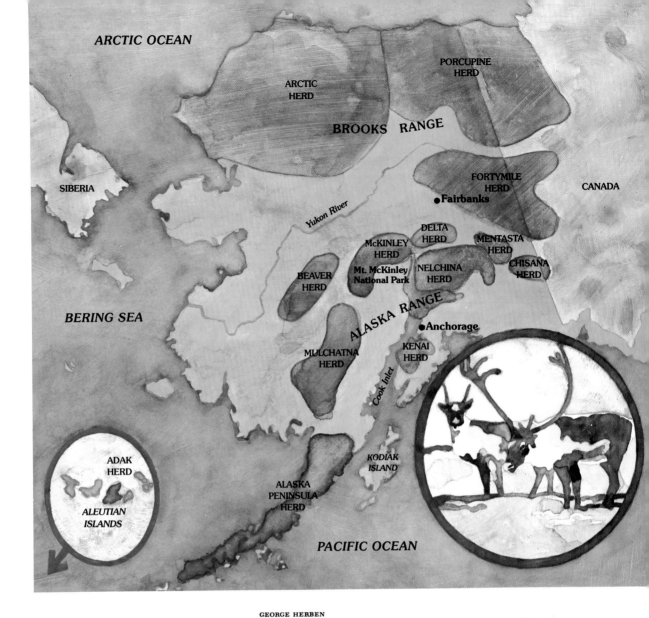

ARCTIC OCEAN

ARCTIC HERD

PORCUPINE HERD

BROOKS RANGE

SIBERIA

FORTYMILE HERD

CANADA

●Fairbanks

Yukon River

DELTA HERD

McKINLEY HERD

MENTASTA HERD

Mt. McKinley National Park

NELCHINA HERD

CHISANA HERD

BEAVER HERD

BERING SEA

ALASKA RANGE

●Anchorage

MULCHATNA HERD

KENAI HERD

Cook Inlet

KODIAK ISLAND

ADAK HERD

ALEUTIAN ISLANDS

ALASKA PENINSULA HERD

PACIFIC OCEAN

MORE THAN 600,000 caribou are distributed throughout the state, except in the Southeastern Panhandle area and on most offshore islands. Major herds are shown above. At left, caribou gather on a snow patch in the Alaska Range in an attempt to find relief from mosquitoes and warble flies that harass them in midsummer.

INTERIOR   **105**

# The Southcentral Region

# Metropolitan center, recreation country, a backdrop of lofty peaks

Half of Alaska's residents live in this region that borders the Gulf of Alaska south of the Alaska Range. Trade, financial, cultural, and social center for the region is the fast-growing city of Anchorage, which enjoys a magnificent setting on a bluff overlooking Cook Inlet. Knik Arm of the inlet curves around the northwestern side of the city. Turnagain Arm cuts inland at the south. To the east, the beautiful Chugach Mountains rise over 8,000 feet. Nestled between these mountains and the Talkeetnas, the fertile Matanuska Valley, settled in 1935 by government-subsidized colonists, is the heartland of Alaska's agricultural industry. Lakes in the valley, some lined with vacation homes, are popular summer and winter playgrounds for Anchorage residents. South of Anchorage, the Seward Highway winds along Turnagain Arm onto the Kenai Peninsula, where old Russian fishing villages contrast with new oil boom towns and a ruggedly beautiful, untracked interior is still wild enough to get lost in. The ice-scoured Kenai Mountains drop to deep glacial fiords on the east side of the peninsula. On the Cook Inlet side, the mountains give way to expanses of forests that roll down to graceful ribbons of beach. On a clear day, you can see the Chigmit Mountains across the water. Good roads link the towns of Southcentral Alaska and connect Anchorage with Fairbanks and the Alaska Highway in the Interior. Anchorage International Airport is a hub for air travel to and from Europe, Asia, Hawaii, the "Lower 48," and the rest of Alaska. The Alaska Railroad, headquartered in Anchorage, provides a 741-mile rail link between the coast and Fairbanks, northern terminus of the line.

KEITH GUNNAR

# From Tent Town Beginnings
## Anchorage is where the people are

*A GROWING ANCHORAGE spreads out on the coastal plain between the Chugach Mountains and Cook Inlet. The downtown buildings rise a little higher every year, and the city continues to reach farther and farther toward the mountain slopes.*

SHIP CREEK LANDING, *tent camp for the Alaska Railroad and forerunner of Anchorage, had a motley population of some 3,000 laborers, gamblers, prostitutes, and legitimate tradespeople when this photograph was taken in 1915. Even its hotel, the Crist House (center of photograph), was housed in an oversized tent.*

# You Can't Stop Alaska's Gardeners
## Greenhouses lend them a helping hand

LENORE HEDLA

LENORE HEDLA

LENORE HEDLA

*INDOOR GARDENING is an Alaskan specialty. Vegetables which would not ripen outdoors during the short growing season thrive in small home greenhouses, and at the Anchorage municipal greenhouses, right, flowers for summer's park plantings get a head start from seed sown in April. A handful of determined gardeners operate their greenhouses all winter—the parka-clad owner of the beautiful orchids above carries water from house to greenhouse when the pipes are drained in winter.*

*SAME GARDEN POND gets winter and summer use.*
*Plastic-lined and filled with water from the owner's well, the frozen pond*
*is used by young hockey players on wintry afternoons. In summer, great*
*beds of annuals create a colorful garden vista.*

ALICE PUSTER

# In Summer, the City Blossoms
## Flowers and flags cheer downtown shoppers

*A GREAT COLOR EXPLOSION brightens downtown Anchorage from mid-July until around Labor Day. Annuals planted out from the city greenhouses thrive in the long hours of daylight and cool summer temperatures.*

NANCY SIMMERMAN

112

*FLAGS FLUTTER in a light summer breeze. The tall pole rising out of photograph was presented by Ketchikan's Chamber of Commerce in 1959. Other flags represent countries whose airlines fly through Anchorage, emphasizing the city's claim to being "Crossroads of the Air World."*

# By Plane, Road, Trail

PHYLLIS ELVING

# Open space is never far away

ANCHORAGE DAILY TIMES PHOTOS BY ALICE PUSTER

*IT'S STILL POSSIBLE to walk a wooded trail through residential Anchorage, or to drive an almost deserted highway into the nearby hills. The two youngsters at left above are headed for adventure along a strip of park land that borders Chester Creek. On a pretty fall day, O'Malley Road at right above has one lone motorist. Opposite, air-minded residents of Anchorage berth their planes on Hood and Spenard lakes (where planes have the right-of-way on adjacent roads).*

*LIKE A HUGE BAKED ALASKA,*
*a snow-covered St. Augustine*
*Island seems to float on the*
*southern waters of Cook Inlet.*
*When the tide goes out at*
*Turnagain Arm, however, the scene*
*more closely resembles chocolate*
*pudding. Tides here range*
*between 30 and 39 feet.*

# An Inlet of Contrasts
## For Captain Cook, it held great promise

*TIDE'S IN, and hopeful salmon fishermen line the shore at the mouth of Bird Creek on Turnagain Arm. The turbulent fiord was wryly named River Turnagain by Captain Cook in 1778 when he was forced to turn back from what he thought was the northwest passage he had been seeking.*

*WHEN THE SHAKING STOPPED, this was part of the scene that faced a sad city. On the disastrous Good Friday of March 27, 1964, Alaska suffered the most severe earthquake recorded on the North American continent in this century. The quake and seismic waves that followed took 115 lives and left 4,500 people homeless along Alaska's southern coast.*

# Earthquake!

## Nature's violence reshaped the land

*NOT A BULB WAS BROKEN in the marquee of the old Denali Theater, right, though the building itself dropped ten feet. Time has softened the raw look of Earthquake Park, below, but you can still stroll paths among upturned slabs of clay and trees that tilt at crazy angles.*

ANCHORAGE DAILY TIMES PHOTO BY ALICE PUSTER

ALICE PUSTER

119

# The Days are Short
## And sports enthusiasts fill them all

ALICE PUSTER

ALICE PUSTER

*SNOW IS NO DETERRENT to the Alaska outdoorsman. "Motor mushers" take to the open spaces by snow machine, and planes exchange wheels or floats for skis to carry snowshoers and skiers to their destinations.*

*ABOVE THE CLOUDS, these three enjoy some weak midday sunshine and the quiet of ski touring at Turnagain Pass.*

NANCY SIMMERMAN

# Lake Attractions North of Anchorage
## There's lots to do when the days lengthen

*THERE'S SOMETHING FOR EVERYONE at Big Lake. The fishermen above seem to find the waters productive, and the sailors should have no complaints about the brisk breeze. In winter, fishermen dip their lines through a frozen surface, and snowmobiles replace the sailboats.*

*BOATING is a leading Big Lake activity. The boats below are using a channel that connects the upper end of the lake with a smaller lake beyond that cannot be reached by road.*

*LONG HOURS OF DAYLIGHT make water skiing possible well into the evening. Calm waters, a beautiful setting, and easy access make Big Lake a favorite recreation spot for Anchorage people, many of whom have cabins around the lake and use them both winter and summer.*

GENTLE FARMLAND is an unexpected change from the rugged mountain scenery that meets the eye almost everywhere in Alaska. Dairying is the leading industry in the Matanuska Valley, but visitors are always fascinated by the vegetables, which range from normal-sized commercial crops to giants like the cabbages at right. A world-record turnip produced in 1968 weighed 50 pounds, and a 73-pound cabbage has been recorded. Of the 202 families who settled the valley in 1935 under a government-sponsored colonization project, only about one-fourth remain, and only about half of those still farm the land.

# Cows and Cabbages

## Quiet pastureland comes as a surprise

*GOLDEN FIELDS and snow-tinged mountains transform the valley when autumn arrives. The Talkeetna and Chugach mountain ranges ring the valley on three sides. At the southwestern end, the valley opens to the coastal plain that edges Cook Inlet.*

# Old-Time Country Fair
## All the sights and sounds and smells are there

*PALMER'S BIG FAIR draws enthusiastic crowds to the Matanuska Valley during its annual pre-Labor Day run. All the sights, sounds, and smells of a country fair are there, including clowns and cotton candy, prize-winning flowers, giant vegetables (the cabbages must weigh 50 pounds even to compete), and homemade berry pies.*

SPECIAL EVENTS *at the Palmer fair include horse shows, livestock judging, and dog obedience trials, and of course no state fair would be complete without its ferris wheel and other midway amusements.*

# Through the Mountains
## Blossoming hillsides, fantastic vistas

*A PURPLE-BLUE BLANKET of lupine colors this hillside along the Richardson Highway in July. One of the showiest of Alaska's wildflowers, it blooms in most of the state and is even found in a miniature version on the barren tundra of the Arctic.*

*A DRIFT OF FLUFFY CLOUDS follows the summit outline of glacier-frosted Mount Drum in the majestic Wrangell Mountains. On a bright, clear day, the mountain seems very near, but it is more than 40 miles away from this small lake near Copper Center.*

# ...through the Mountains

ICY STREAMS *lure fishermen and present obstacles to hikers. The angler at left is trying his luck on a tributary of the Copper River. Above, a hiker takes the chancy way across a rivulet in Matanuska Glacier.*

A CURTAIN OF WATER *plunges down a rocky slope to the Lowe River that parallels the Richardson Highway on the way to Valdez. This is Horsetail Falls, one of several lovely cascades south of Thompson Pass.*

# Mining Ghosts
## Quiet descended when the mines closed down

ABANDONED NOW, Kennecott's barn-red buildings, giant mill and company stores, warehouses and homes, perch on the edge of a glacier five road miles from McCarthy. At the head of the valley, the summit of Mount Blackburn, highest of the Wrangell Mountains, is brilliant in its white covering of snow. Kennecott produced almost a quarter of a billion dollars in copper ore before the supply was exhausted and the mines closed down in 1938.

GEORGE HERBEN

GEORGE HERBEN

*TIRED BUILDINGS and a few sad relics like the one at left are reminders of the lusty, brawling camp of Chitina which served the Kennecott mines. Today, ghost town buffs are drawn to the almost deserted town, where the general store is still doing business and a fascinating museum overflows with relics of Chitina's livelier past.*

# Through Canyons
## Roads and rivers, and now the pipe

JEFF PHILLIPS

ED COOPER

WALLS OF PIPE form this man-made canyon at the port of Valdez. Eight hundred miles of the 48-inch pipe are waiting to carry the North Slope oil from Prudhoe Bay to Valdez via a route that will cross the Chugach Mountains at Thompson Pass, then descend through Keystone Canyon (left).

RICHARDSON HIGHWAY
and the Lowe River follow
the steep-walled chasm of
Keystone Canyon near Valdez.

SOUTHCENTRAL   **135**

# Serene in Any Season
## There's quiet at the end of the roads

*VALDEZ INLET sparkles in its winter setting. The scene here followed by several months that first light snowfall of the season, referred to by Alaskans as "Termination Dust"—a sign that summer is at an end.*

*A PEACEFUL PLACE to while away an hour or so, McKinley Lake awaits the hiker at the end of a short trail from the Copper River road.*

*BY HIKING TRAILS, you reach the heart of mountains that often seem quite remote as you travel Alaska's main roads. The trail to McKinley Lake leads through this peaceful forest.*

# A Setting to Marvel At

*WHEN ALASKA'S SKIES ARE CLEAR, moon and stars seem incredibly bright, and when the beautiful mountains near Valdez are bathed in the light from an enormous full moon, it's easy to understand why many people consider this to be one of the most beautiful parts of the state.*

# By night or by day, the view fascinates

*THREATENING SKIES keep small craft tucked safely behind the protective breakwater at Cordova's harbor. Now reached only by boat or plane, Cordova will eventually have a road connection to the Richardson Highway via a route through the Copper and Tasnuna river valleys.*

# Prince William Sound
## A popular loop by road, water, and rail

YOU DRIVE ABOARD *the ferry for the seven-hour crossing of Prince William Sound, then relax in your car during the 35-minute rail trip through the mountains to Portage. In either direction, you can work out a delightfully scenic, 450-mile loop trip from Anchorage.*

*THROUGH ICY WATERS, the ferry glides toward Columbia Glacier,
highlight of the Valdez-Whittier trip. One of Alaska's largest tidewater
glaciers, the Columbia flows for 41 miles out of the Chugach Mountains.*

# The Kenai is Vacation Country
## Favorite destination...for a weekend, a week, or longer

GLENN M. CHRISTIANSEN

*UNCROWDED CAMPGROUNDS, with lakes, streams, and trails nearby, lure vacationers who wish to extend their Kenai stay for longer than the usual brief tour. Family here has stopped for a lunch break at Tern Lake, named for the Arctic terns that nest there each summer.*

*VISITOR GETS HELP from this prospector near Hope who has been digging for gold on and off since 1910 and still works a claim on Resurrection Creek. Below, hikers near the end of the seven-mile trail to Lost Lake near Seward, a trail that climbs gently from dense coastal forest to above timberline.*

# ...The Kenai

*CLAM TIDE! When the word goes out, hundreds of hopeful clam diggers flock to Clam Gulch in search of the succulent razors. During a good clam tide, the beach population sometimes nears 1,500, and on one especially good day, an estimated 50,000 clams were dug.*

ED COOPER

*RESURRECTION BAY at Seward is famous for sport fishing. Silver salmon generally start running in late July and continue through September. In the annual Silver Salmon Derby about mid-August, lucky anglers may win anywhere from $100 to $3,000.*

# By Canoe Trail through a Wilderness

JEFF PHILLIPS

GLENN M. CHRISTIANSEN

*THE KENAI BACK COUNTRY,*
*inaccessible by road, offers a*
*quiet experience. Winding through*
*the northern part of the Kenai*
*Moose Range, marked canoe trails,*
*varying in difficulty from "beginner"*
*to "expert," follow rivers and lakes*
*connected by short portages. The*
*Swanson River system links more than*
*40 lakes along the Swanson River; the*
*Swan Lake route connects 30 lakes*
*on forks of the Moose River.*

# Moose and people share the lakes

*THIS IS MOOSE COUNTRY, and anywhere along the way, you're apt to be watched by one of these ungainly—and curious—members of the deer family, who find food and protection in the thick stands of spruce, birch, and aspen, and hundreds of tiny lakes and streams.*

# Onion-domed Churches
## Sightseers find them irresistible

*A SINGLE ONION DOME and Russian cross mark this abandoned, weathered chapel in Kenai. Present-day Kenai is on the site of old Fort Saint Nicholas (1791), a fur trading post that was the second permanent settlement established by the Russians in Alaska.*

*ATOP A HILL behind Ninilchik, this picturesque Russian church and
cemetery never fail to attract photographers. From the hilltop, you can
look down on the tiny village at the mouth of the Ninilchik River.
On a clear day, the Chigmit Mountains come into view across Cook Inlet.*

# It's Fishing Country
## Some fish for pleasure, some for profit

PHILIP HYDE

*A SALMON RUN off Homer Spit brings crowds of fishermen to the long, narrow bar of gravel that juts into Kachemak Bay at the end of the Sterling Highway. When the fishing is good, the road onto the spit is solidly lined with cars, campers, and trailers.*

FRESHLY CAUGHT shrimp
are hefted onto the cannery
scales at Homer. Commercial
fishing boats at Homer
bring in shrimp, king crab,
halibut, and salmon.

NO ROADS lead to Seldovia,
a small fishing village across
the bay from Homer. Access is by
plane or ferry. Before the 1964
earthquake, much of the old town
was built on pilings above the
water. Following the quake, the
town underwent a remodeling, but
much of its old charm remains.

# ...Fishing Country

*A GOOD CATCH of salmon rewards the sport fishermen at left and the commercial fisherman above. On a sparkling September day, Ptarmigan Creek, below, lures hopeful anglers.*

*PERHAPS A NIBBLE from a rainbow or Dolly Varden will interrupt the quiet of this scene on Jean Lake, but now the only sounds are the lapping of water and the rustling of birch leaves stirred by a gentle breeze.*

# The Southwestern Corner

# Willawaws and wildlife, a unique national monument, fog-shrouded volcanoes

Weather is made in this slender curve of Alaska that stretches for some 2,000 miles into the Pacific Ocean. Storms spawned here, where the warm waters of the Pacific meet the cold Bering Sea, affect the weather in all of North America. The native population of this southwestern corner is made up of Aleuts, who are related to the Eskimos but who have customs, traditions, and a language of their own. Kodiak, where the Russians had their first permanent settlement in the New World, is still the largest town. West of Kodiak Island, at the northeastern end of the Alaska Peninsula, remote Katmai National Monument, largest national monument in the United States, protects an immense and almost untouched wilderness of forests, fish-filled lakes and streams, ocean bays and lagoons, and the famous "Valley of Ten Thousand Smokes," site of one of the most violent volcanic eruptions in history. Beyond the Alaska Peninsula, the barren, wind-swept Aleutian Islands stretch in a curving chain for about 1,500 miles. Attu, westernmost of the group, is almost directly above New Zealand. Far out on the chain are radar installations, weather stations, airports, and isolated supply and fish-processing settlements. Most of the islands are part of the Aleutian Islands National Wildlife Refuge. Kelp beds are home to sea otters, and flocks of sea birds swirl above nesting areas on beaches and rugged cliffs. Some 250 miles north of the Aleutians, the Pribilof Islands are the breeding grounds of the fur seal, hunted almost to extinction in the early part of this century. Now under international protection, a herd of over 1¼ million of these animals arrives on the tiny islands each summer after a swim of over 5,000 miles from warmer waters.

ROBERT C. REEVE

# Kodiak is Where It All Began
## Furs were the prize then, the sea provides today

CLIFF HOLLENBECK

*DELIGHTFULLY UNSPOILED Kodiak nestles at the foot of Pillar Mountain on an isolated island chosen by the Russians as the site of their first permanent settlement in Alaska. Furs were the prize then. Today, the Kodiak fishing fleet, largest in Alaska, sails out from a quiet harbor, and sixteen canneries in town process their catch.*

*ONION-DOMED CHURCH, rebuilt after the original burned in 1943, is a reminder of the Russian past and an active part of the present.*

*RUSSIAN INFLUENCE shows in Kodiak street names and in the faces of many of the people you will meet around town.*

# Torches Flare, Cannons Boom
## And the story of a stubborn, ingenious, dedicated man unfolds

158

*HISTORY COMES TO LIFE
for an exciting few days
each August when Kodiak's
residents stage the stirring
production, "Cry of the Wild
Ram." Cannons boom from the
beach near the amphitheater, an
answering volley comes from
the darkness of Monashka Bay,
and the audience sits spellbound
as the drama unfolds. Almost 200
Kodiak residents participate
as actors and behind-the-scenes
workers in staging the
epic-drama, which tells of
Alexander Baranof's struggle to
carve a Russian empire in
this untamed part of the world.*

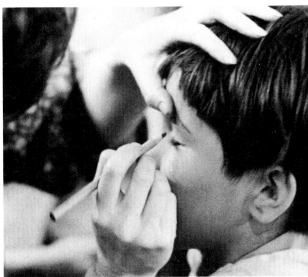

# Civilization is Far Behind

NANCY SIMMERMAN

*BEAR TRAIL, above, meanders through the still forest near Brooks River in Katmai National Monument. It was worn into the forest floor by the huge brown bears that roam the wilderness of southwestern Alaska. At right, a lone kayaker enjoys the late-afternoon quiet on Naknek Lake in the heart of this beautiful, unspoiled land.*

# Trails are made by bears, and a man can be alone

# A Mountain Blew Its Top
## In one incredible day, a landscape was transformed

JEFF PHILLIPS

*AN ASH-BURIED VALLEY lies below these hikers in Katmai National Monument. Earth-shaking fireworks led to the establishment of this federal preserve where, on June 6, 1912, a thunderous blast spewed forth masses of pumice and rock fragments from Novarupta Volcano. Some of the more than 7 cubic miles of volcanic material hurled into the atmosphere was carried by winds to all parts of the northern hemisphere.*

*A JADE-GREEN LAKE
fills the crater that
was formed when the top
of Mount Katmai collapsed
during the 1912 volcanic
activity. The collapse
came when molten andesite
beneath the mountaintop
drained away through newly
created fissures, leaving
Katmai's summit unsupported.
At left, hikers look out over
a steep-sided stream channel
cut through volcanic tuff
that covered the valley to
depths as great as 700 feet.*

REWARDS ARE GREAT for the fishermen who wade the snow-fed streams and crystal-clear lakes of the Alaska Peninsula. One of the greatest attractions is the sight of determined salmon (below left) leaping six to eight-foot falls on the Brooks River as they fight their way upstream to their spawning ground.

# Fish Enough for Everyone
Crystal clear lakes, snow-fed streams, and fellow anglers that demand respect

*NOW YOU SEE IT, now you don't! It's a test of speed when fast-moving salmon meets fast-moving bear. In this case, the salmon was the loser, and mother bear and her cubs are happily enjoying the fruits of a successful McNeil River fishing expedition. Largest of all bears, the brown bear of southwestern Alaska may tower nine feet tall when he rears up. Some weigh as much as 1,500 pounds.*

# A Crescent of Volcanoes
## They divide the warm Pacific from the chilly Bering Sea

*WATERFALLS NEVER DRY UP on the moisture-laden Aleutian Islands. The 1,500-mile-long chain of about 40 major islands and many small islands and rocky islets divides the North Pacific from the Bering Sea. Storms born here, where the cold air from the north meets the warm Japanese current, affect the weather of the entire continent.*

KANAGA VOLCANO *makes a brief appearance through ever-present clouds. Nature was violent in her creation of this land, which continues to have some of the most intense volcanic activity in the world. Ten peaks in the range reach above 4,000 feet. Highest is 9,372-foot Mt. Shishaldin on Unimak Island at the eastern end of the chain.*

# ...Aleutian Islands

*COMPLETELY ISOLATED from the rest of the world except for radio communication and the Navy boat that arrives every six weeks, tiny Atka village at the edge of Nazan Bay is a lonely place indeed. The few Aleuts who live on the usually fog-blanketed island subsist largely on their catch of fish, sea mammals, reindeer, and birds.*

*A RARE DAY* on Adak brings a bit of blue to the sky and a touch
of weak sunshine to make the green hillsides look even greener. Frequently
buffeted by gale winds and driving rainstorms, called "willawaws," Adak
has a far from friendly climate but is important as a military outpost.

# An Almost Forgotten Art
## Few find time to become proficient

*A DYING ART is being kept alive by a few dedicated women who still make Aleut baskets and teach basketry to young people. The superb examples below are from a collection donated to the University of Alaska Museum.*

UNIVERSITY OF ALASKA MUSEUM PHOTOS

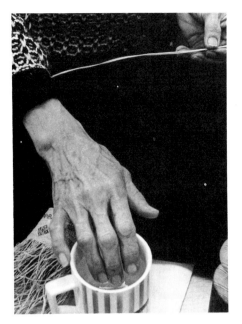 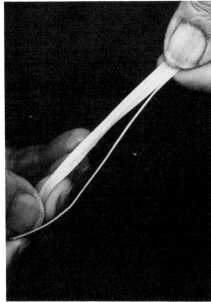 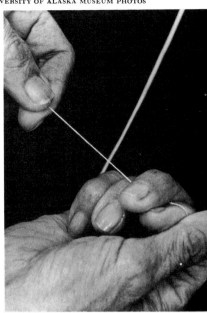

*EACH BLADE OF GRASS selected must be moistened to make it flexible. The moistened grass is split into the proper thickness with the thumb nail, then twisted to improve its strength. So fine was the texture of Aleut baskets that the Russians compared it with that of cloth.*

*DESIGN IS CREATED by twisting embroidery thread over grass strands. (Rubber band is used above to show technique.) Center photo: bottom of basket is woven almost entirely by touch since grasses are between the weaver and her hands. Wooden mold, right, keeps basket in shape when not being worked on.*

# The Wind-swept Pribilofs

# The beaches may be crowded, or you may find yourself alone

*FROM WARMER WATERS off northern Japan and southern California, fur seals begin to arrive at their breeding grounds in the Pribilofs in May. First to arrive are the massive bulls, who stake out their territories on the rocky beaches. In June the first females arrive, and the bulls begin to assemble their 30 to 40-cow harems. The herd begins its long swim south in October, and by the end of the year, the beaches are snow-covered and deserted. The beachcomber above is on a treasure hunt near the small community of Aleuts who live on St. Paul. On the opposite shore of this island, the land drops off in sharp cliffs dotted with bird rookeries. The Pribilofs include St. George, St. Paul, Otter Island, and two small islets.*

# Eskimo Alaska

# Remote villages, permafrost and fragile tundra, an ice-choked sea

The Bering Sea and Arctic Ocean coastlines are about as harsh an area for human life as this planet has to offer. Windy, treeless wastes, where temperatures are well below zero in the winter and rarely above 50 degrees during the brief summer, present what seems to be an almost insurmountable challenge to the ingenuity of man. Yet for centuries, this has been the home of Alaska's remarkable Eskimo people. No roads lead to this part of the state. Scheduled air carriers serve the few major communities, and bush planes reach tiny isolated villages. The old gold rush camp of Nome on the Seward Peninsula is tourist and trade center for northwestern Alaska and the most widely known town. Alaska's Little Diomede Island, off the tip of the peninsula, is separated by only three miles from Russia's Big Diomede Island. On a clear day, you can see mountains in Siberia from Cape Prince of Wales, westernmost tip of the mainland. The northern third of Alaska is within the Arctic Circle. Its shores, washed by the Arctic Ocean, are ice-locked from seven to eight months of the year. For two months each summer, the sun never dips below the horizon, and for two months in winter, the Arctic is in darkness. Principal towns are Kotzebue and Barrow. Point Barrow is the very top of North America—only 1,300 miles from the North Pole. This part of Alaska has been in the news spotlight since explorations in 1968 and 1969 discovered some of the biggest deposits of oil and natural gas in the world beneath the vast expanses of tundra on the North Slope. The way of the Eskimo is undergoing dramatic change. Yet old ways linger on. Many Eskimos still fish and hunt and trap, as in the past, but today they do it with the help of outboard motors and snowmobiles. Hunting and fishing still provide much of the subsistence and economy, and in spring, entire villages turn out at the cry of "Whale!"

# Meeting Place for Water Birds
## Some stay the winter, some roam a third of the world

*A CLOUD OF SNOW GEESE patterns the Yukon Delta en route from nesting grounds in Siberia. The flats of the Yukon River and the delta at its mouth are the two richest waterfowl-producing habitats in Alaska. Each area sends over two million birds south every fall.*

ROCKY ISLANDS and coastal plains are nesting sites for millions of birds. Murres, left, range throughout the northern sea. Below, a spirited emperor goose guards its nest on the Yukon delta, breeding grounds for 90 percent of the world's emperor geese.

177

BETWEEN FLIGHTS,
bush pilot chats with
waiting passengers
at Hooper Bay.

SUPPLIES, mail, and passengers
come and go by plane. Flights
run winter and summer, with a
growing number of engineers,
scientists, government employees,
and sightseers joining the
local passengers.

A SPECIAL SLOT separates
bush mail from other mail at
Nome post office. Nome,
Kotzebue, Fairbanks, and Bethel
are major take-off points
for bush flights.

# Realm of the Bush Pilot

## Where roads don't reach, the bush plane is a vital link

CLIFF HOLLENBECK

*TULUKSAK VILLAGERS turn out to greet the plane. Passengers and crew can always count on a friendly "hello" at each stop. There are usually half a dozen smiling children checking on the new arrivals, and there's plenty of help when it comes to unloading supplies from "outside."*

# A Misty Sanctuary

## These inhabitants are at home in the chill

JERRY HOUT

*THREE SHAGGY MUSK OXEN present a formidable array of horns to the intruding photographer. Eskimos call the animal "Oomingmuk," or "bearded one." Hunted to extinction in Alaska in the last century, the musk ox was reintroduced by transplants from Greenland in the early 1930s. Now, a sizeable herd roams bleak Nunivak Island, protected from the cold by their thick undercoats of soft, cashmere-like "qiviut" and by outer coats of long, coarse hair three feet or more in length. The qiviut, gathered each spring, to be hand-carded and spun into yarn for clothing, is providing a growing source of income for island residents.*

JERRY HOUT

*REINDEER ROUND-UP is an annual event on Nunivak Island. This domesticated relative of the caribou was introduced into Alaska from Siberia around the turn of the century.*

JERRY HOUT

*HAPPILY FREE from the tagging procedure, reindeer bound from the sorting chute, ready to join the rest of the Nunivak herd, which now numbers over 10,000.*

# Long Winter Ahead

RUTH KIRK

*PTARMIGAN will supplement a diet of fish and caribou for these ladies, just back from a successful hunting expedition near their Kobuk River village. Birds were captured by snares set up in willows. Between the once-a-year barge visit, families here subsist on what they can get by hunting, fishing, and trapping.*

# The land provides for those who make the effort

SNOWMOBILE, left, is being readied to haul caribou-laden sled back to village. Winter's meat supply, caught when herd comes through, will be tossed on house roofs, where freezing temperatures will preserve it until needed.
In some places, subterranean caches, carved out of permafrost, serve as storage areas. Family below, one of few who have not converted to oil or natural gas for heating and cooking, has stacked an adequate wood supply.

183

PRESSURE RIDGE, above, is vantage point for hunters, who sometimes walk 12 miles or more in a single day in their hunt for game, such as the polar bear who left his tracks on the ice, below left. Eskimo crew, below right, on lookout for seals and walrus, guides umiak through moving ice.

# Hunters of the Bering Sea
## Travel here is a calculated risk

*WALRUS HIDE is split to get proper thickness for covering umiak frame. It will take this woman all day, using "ulu" (woman's knife), to complete the task. Skin covering on umiak is replaced every two years.*

*CAUTIOUS HUNTERS approach resting pod of walrus. Eskimos use every part of the walrus kill. Meat and innards will be eaten or fed to dogs; skin will become umiak covering; ivory will be used for carving. Even clams from walrus stomach will be cleaned, boiled, and served for supper.*

# Christmas is Special Here

## A community welcome greets Santa in his own territory

NED HAINES

*UNDAUNTED BY WINTER DARKNESS, residents of the Eskimo village of Point Hope at the edge of the Chukchi Sea brave Arctic cold to hold the sled dog races that are a part of their annual Christmas festivities.*

OPERATION SANTA CLAUS is a project of Alaska's Air National Guard. Toys, food, clothing, and even Santa Claus arrive by plane at the isolated village of St. Mary's near the mouth of the Yukon. Everyone turns out for the Christmas program at the schoolhouse, where choral arrangements and native dances are enthusiastically presented by students of the mission school.

ANCHORAGE DAILY TIMES PHOTOS BY ALICE PUSTER

ESKIMO ALASKA **187**

# Frozen Water, Frozen Ground
## Ice leaves its mark on land and sea

PETER G. SANCHEZ

*A MIDNIGHT SUN casts a warm glow over the ice-choked sea at Kotzebue. Photographs on opposite page show Arctic tundra, the thin layer of life-supporting vegetation above permanently frozen subsoil (permafrost). From top to bottom: strange patterns (polygons) form on tundra when ground contracts and cracks in intense cold; water, unable to penetrate permafrost layer, remains on surface in hundreds of tiny ponds; ice layer beneath tundra pushes soil upward; deep-cut bank of Kobuk River shows thin layer of tundra, which supports spindly, shallow-rooted trees.*

ESKIMO ALASKA    **189**

# Gold Colored the Sands

*A NOW-DESERTED BEACH edges the southern shore of the Seward Peninsula at Nome, where only rusting machinery and an occasional lone beachcomber interrupt a monotonous stretch of sand that once lured thousands of gold-hungry prospectors.*

# After the Klondike, gold fever reached to the sea

GRAINS OF GOLD and an audience of interested bystanders rewarded miners who patiently panned Nome's beach sand. The beach strike, which lured thousands to Nome in the summer of 1900, was quickly exhausted, but large mining companies continued operations on the Seward Peninsula for the next five years.

# ...Nome

*TENTS AND SUPPLIES were scattered for miles along Nome's beach. New arrivals were brought by barge as close to shore as possible, then had to wade the remaining distance.*

*HOPEFUL AMATEURS learn the technique of gold-panning near Nome. The idle dredge stands as a reminder of busier days. Only two commercial dredges operate in Alaska now, but smaller ones are active from time to time.*

# The Dances Tell the Stories
## Fanciful props make them more convincing

*YOUNG AND OLD participate in Eskimo dances, standard entertainment for almost every visitor to the Arctic. Parkas, headdresses, feathers, and masks are colorful embellishments to dance routines.*

*SIMPLE MOVEMENTS*
*pantomime stories that tell*
*of whale hunts, courting*
*of a maiden, taking of a wife.*
*Chanting and drum beats*
*provide the musical*
*accompaniment. Traditional*
*drum was made of skin; some*
*newer ones are of plastic.*

195

# Summer Enlivens the Arctic
## Long days bring a flurry of activity

*A SEA BREEZE freshens a colorful array of laundry strung on lines along Kotzebue's beach. Snowmobiles are put aside for bicycles, and everyone turns out to enjoy this all-too-brief time of long, sun-lit days.*

*BLANKET TOSS is fun
for everyone. Visitors
are welcome to try
this stunt, but local
youngsters are the
chief participants.*

*SUMMER FUN is where
you find it. It may be
dipping a line, looking
for beach treasures,
or enjoying a ride on
an improvised swing.*

ESKIMO ALASKA **197**

# ...Arctic Summer

*SUMMER CAMPS,
set up on the tundra,
are centers for berrying,
fishing, hunting. Now
and then, a brave swimmer
takes a plunge, but the
stay is usually brief.*

*A GOOD HAUL of fish will provide food
for the months to come. Woman at left is using
ulu to split salmon for drying on racks (above).*

# The Fragile Tundra

WALTER R. SPOFFORD

*SOFT LIGHT OF EVENING bathes the tundra near the Colville River.
In summer, tundra layer thaws and becomes spongy, but permafrost beneath
remains at below-freezing temperature. State law prohibits driving on
tundra during summer thaw because tire tracks become permanent scars.*

# Seemingly uninhabited, but watch where you step!

*ALMOST UNNOTICED, peregrine falcon eggs lie well-camouflaged on river bank; young rough-legged hawks begin their explorations; perky Arctic poppies reach for the fleeting sunlight; and a downy snowy owlet peers warily from its tundra home.*

# Top of the Continent
## Isolated settlements survive on a stark Arctic shore

*LARGEST ESKIMO SETTLEMENT in Alaska, Barrow occupies a bleak setting at the edge of the ice-choked sea. The ice pack moves in and out seasonally and with the changing winds. Natural gas heats most of the houses, but Barrow living is still primitive by "outside" standards.*

WHALE BLUBBER AND WHALE BONES *are put to good use. Above, blocks of muktuk (rubbery skin of whale with layer of blubber attached), considered a delicacy by Eskimos, are dragged away after whale butchering on Point Hope beach. Decorative attempts use whatever is at hand: whale vertebrae serve the purpose around Barrow church sign, below.*

# Village on a Moonscape

LAEL MORGAN

*LONELY ANAKTUVUK PASS, home of Alaska's only remaining group of inland Eskimos, cuts through bleak, almost uninhabited Brooks Range of northern Alaska.*

# Selected Readings

This bibliography is not intended to be a complete listing of books on Alaskan subjects. It is limited to fairly recent books that are of an informative nature and are likely to be found in most large libraries and good bookstores. It does not include fiction, magazines, pamphlets, or out-of-print books.

## Books of General Interest

Becker, Ethel A. *A Treasury of Alaskana*. Seattle; Superior Publishing Company, 1969.

———. *Klondike '98*. Portland; Binfords & Mort, 1967.

Berton, Pierre. *Klondike Fever*. Westminster, Md.; Alfred A. Knopf, Inc., 1958.

Brower, Charles D. *Fifty Years Below Zero*. New York; Dodd, Mead & Co., 1942.

Brown, Dale. *Wild Alaska*. New York; Time-Life Books, 1972.

Day, Beth. *Glacier Pilot*. New York; Holt, Rinehart and Winston, 1957.

DeArmond, R.N. *'Stroller' White: Tales of a Klondike Newsman*. Vancouver, Canada; Mitchell Press Limited, 1969.

Fish, Byron et al. *Eskimo Boy Today*. Anchorage; Alaska Northwest Publishing Co., 1971.

Green, Paul. *I Am Eskimo: Aknik My Name*. Anchorage; Alaska Northwest Publishing Co., 1959.

Gruening, Ernest. *An Alaskan Reader*. New York; Meredith Press, 1966.

———. *Many Battles: The Autobiography of Ernest Gruening*. New York; Liveright Publishing Corp., 1973.

———. *The State of Alaska*. New York; Random House, Inc., 1968.

Herbert, Wally. *Across the Top of the World*. New York; G. P. Putnam's Sons, 1971.

Herndon, Booton. *The Great Land*. New York; Weybright & Talley, Inc., 1971.

Jenness, Aylette. *Dwellers of the Tundra: Life in an Alaskan Eskimo Village*. Riverside, N.J.; Macmillan, Inc., 1970.

Keating, Bern. *Alaska*. Washington, D.C.; National Geographic Society, 1969.

Keith, Ronald A. *Bush Pilot with a Briefcase*. Garden City, N.Y.; Doubleday & Company, Inc., 1972.

Keith, Sam. *One Man's Wilderness*. Anchorage; Alaska Northwest Publishing Co., 1973.

Laycock, George. *Alaska: The Embattled Frontier*. New York; Houghton Mifflin Co., 1971.

Martinsen, Ella L. *Black Sand and Gold*. Portland; Binfords & Mort, 1967.

Mills, Stephen. *Arctic War Birds*. Seattle; Superior Publishing Company, 1971.

Mills, Stephen E., and Phillips, James W. *Sourdough Sky*. Seattle; Superior Publishing Company, 1969.

Milton, John P. *Nameless Valleys, Shining Mountains*. New York; Walker & Company, 1970.

Murie, Margaret. *Two in the Far North*. Westminster, Md.; Alfred A. Knopf, Inc., 1962.

Murie, Olaus J. *Journeys to the Far North*. Palo Alto, Calif.; American West Publishing Company, 1973.

Reynolds, Robert. *Alaska*. Portland; Charles H. Belding, 1971.

Rogers, George W. *Alaska in Transition*. Baltimore; Johns Hopkins University Press, 1960.

———. *Change in Alaska: People, Petroleum, and Politics*. Seattle; University of Washington Press, 1970.

———. *Future of Alaska*, Baltimore; Johns Hopkins University Press, 1962.

Satterfield, Archie, and Jarman, Lloyd. *Alaska Bush Pilots in the Float Country*. Seattle; Superior Publishing Company, 1969.

Smith, Richard Austin. *The Frontier States*. New York; Time-Life Books, 1968.

Spring, Bob and Ira, and Fish, Byron. *Alaska*. Seattle; Superior Publishing Company, 1970.

Thomas, Tay. *Only in Alaska*. Garden City, N.Y.; Doubleday & Company, Inc., 1969.

Walker, Franklin. *Jack London and the Klondike*. San Marino, Calif; Huntington Library Publications, 1966.

Wright, Billie. *Four Seasons North*. Scranton, Pa.; Harper & Row Publishers, Inc., 1973.

## Historical Works

Bancroft, H. H. *History of Alaska, 1730-1885*. New York; Hafner Press, 1970.

Barry, Mary J. *A History of Mining on the Kenai Peninsula*. Anchorage; Alaska Northwest Publishing Co., 1973.

Chevigny, Hector. *Lord of Alaska*. Portland; Binfords & Mort, 1970.

———. *Russian America*. New York; Viking Press, Inc., 1965.

Neatby, L. H. *Conquest of the Last Frontier*. Athens; Ohio University Press, 1968.

Satterfield, Archie. *Chilkoot Pass, Then and Now*. Anchorage; Alaska Northwest Publishing Co., 1973.

Shiels, Archie W. *The Purchase of Alaska*. Seattle; University of Washington Press, 1967.

Gruening, Ernest. *The Battle for Alaska Statehood*. Seattle; University of Washington Press, 1967.

Hulley, Clarence C. *Alaska: Past and Present.* Portland; Binfords & Mort, 1970.

Naske, Claus M. *An Interpretative History of Alaskan Statehood.* Anchorage; Alaska Northwest Publishing Co., 1973.

Sherwood, Morgan B. *Exploration of Alaska 1865-1900.* New Haven; Yale University Press, 1965.

Wood, James P. *Alaska: The Great Land.* New York; Hawthorn Books, Inc., 1967.

## Specialized Subjects

Bandi, Hans-Georg. *Eskimo Prehistory.* College; University of Alaska Press, 1969.

Bank, Ted II. *People of the Bering Sea.* New York; MSS Educational Publishing Co., 1967.

Birket-Smith, Kaj. *Eskimos.* New York; Crown Publishers, Inc., 1971.

Bohn, Dave. *Glacier Bay: The Land and the Silence.* San Francisco; Sierra Club, 1967.

Bruemmer, Fred. *Seasons of the Eskimo.* Greenwich, Conn.; New York Graphic Society Ltd., 1971.

Chance, Norman. *Eskimo of North Alaska.* New York; Holt, Rinehart & Winston, 1966.

Chasan, Daniel Jack. *Klondike '70: The Alaskan Oil Boom.* New York; Praeger Publishers, 1971.

Collins, Henry B. et al. *The Far North: 2000 Years of American Eskimo and Indian Art.* Washington; National Gallery of Art, 1973.

Drucker, Philip. *Indians of the Northwest Coast.* Garden City, N.Y.; Natural History Press, 1963.

Fejes, Clarie. *People of the Noatak.* New York; Alfred A. Knopf, 1970.

Fitch, Edwin M. *The Alaska Railroad.* New York; Praeger Publishers, 1967.

Garfield, Viola E., and Forrest, Linn A. *The Wolf and the Raven.* Seattle; University of Washington Press, 1961.

Garfield, Viola E., and Wingert, Paul S. *Tsimshian Indians & Their Arts.* Seattle; University of Washington Press, 1966.

Giddings, J. L. *Ancient Men of the Arctic.* Westminster, Md.; Alfred A. Knopf, Inc., 1967.

————. *Kobuk River People.* College; University of Alaska Press, 1970.

Keim, Charles J. *Aghvook, White Eskimo: Otto Geist & Alaskan Archeology.* College; University of Alaska Press, 1969.

Keithahn, Edward L. *Monuments in Cedar.* Seattle; Superior Publishing Company, 1963.

Krause, Aurel. *The Tlingit Indians.* Seattle; University of Washington Press, 1970.

Lantis, Margaret. *Alaskan Eskimo Ceremonialism.* Seattle; University of Washington Press, 1947.

Marshall, Robert. *Alaska Wilderness: Exploring the Central Brooks Range.* Berkeley; University of California Press, 1970.

Martin, Cy. *Gold Rush Narrow Gauge.* Los Angeles; Trans-Anglo Books, 1969.

Mathews, Richard. *The Yukon.* New York; Holt, Rinehart and Winston, 1968.

McFeat, Tom. *Indians of the North Pacific Coast.* Seattle; University of Washington Press, 1967.

Morgan, Murray. *One Man's Gold Rush.* Seattle; University of Washington Press, 1967.

Murie, Adolph. *A Naturalist in Alaska.* New York; Devin-Adair Co., 1961.

————. *Birds of Mount McKinley: A field handbook.* McKinley Park; Mount McKinley Natural History Association, 1963.

————. *Mammals of Mount McKinley.* McKinley Park; Mount McKinley Natural History Association, 1962.

Nelson, Richard K. *Hunters of the Northern Ice.* Chicago; University of Chicago Press, 1969.

Oswalt, Wendell H. *Alaskan Eskimos.* Scranton, Pa.; Chandler Publishing Company, 1967.

Phillips, James W. *Alaska-Yukon Place Names.* Seattle; University of Washington Press, 1973.

Ray, Dorothy Jean. *Artists of the Tundra and the Sea.* Seattle; University of Washington Press, 1961.

Sage, Bryan L. *Alaska and Its Wildlife.* New York; Viking Press, Inc., 1973.

Salisbury, O. M. *Quoth the Raven.* Seattle; Superior Publishing Company, 1963.

Sheldon, Charles. *The Wilderness of Denali.* New York; Charles Scribner's Sons, 1960.

Stonehouse, Bernard. *Animals of the Arctic: the ecology of the Far North.* New York; Holt, Rinehart and Winstone, 1971.

## Guide Books

Montague, Richard W. *Exploring Mount McKinley National Park.* Anchorage; Alaska Travel Publications, Inc., 1973.

Spring, Norma. *Alaska: The Complete Travel Book.* New York; Macmillan, Inc., 1970.

Sunset Editors. *Alaska.* Menlo Park, Calif.; Lane Magazine & Book Company, 1966.

*The Milepost.* Anchorage; Alaska Northwest Publishing Co., rev. annually.

Washburn, Bradford. *A Tourist Guide to Mount McKinley.* Anchorage; Alaska Northwest Publishing Co., 1971.

# Index

This book was printed and bound by Kingsport Press, Kingsport, Tennessee, from litho film prepared by Graphics Arts Center, Portland, Oregon. Body type is Palatino composed by Continental Graphics, Los Angeles, California; heads are Palatino composed by Continental Graphics, Los Angeles, California, and Souvenir composed by Timely Typography, San Francisco, California. Paper for pages is by Westvaco, Luke, Maryland.